MINDSET

10 Mindset Tricks to Master
the Power of Positive Thinking
Free Your Mind and Achieve
Success Today

By JOANNE ROBINSON

Table of Contents

Chapter 1: Mindset - A Determinant of Your Victory

Humans are different from all other creatures because of their ability to pursue mental and intellectual tasks. Although, animals and living creatures are also bestowed with the ability to analyze the surrounding and make decisions, yet the human intellect has no match. The abilities of animals may be related to survival needs only, but those of humans are aimed at creating miracles in their life. It is the human intellect which has made him conquer the universe in the form of inventions and discoveries.

The mental abilities of humans are one of the most complex topics, which have attracted hundreds of researches and discoveries. It is because of its complex nature which depends upon various dispositional and situational factors. As far as the mental models of human mind are concerned, the subjective phenomenon of "mindset" appears as one of the multifaceted domain of human mind.

Mindset:

"It denotes a set of fixed attitudes, view, opinions and behaviors which are driven by the cognitive processing and ensuring signals."

The definition claims that because of the cognitive processing our ideas and opinions are reflected through our behaviors. It is because of this reason that we want to study mindset so that the eventual behaviors can be made ideal or, at least, close to ideal.

In human psychology and cognitive studies, nothing is ideal. It varies from person to person and depends on situational context. Yet the experts want to modify the mindset in such a way that humans can live a healthy and enthusiastic life.

Performance loop is driven by Mindset:

The eventual loop of mindset, involving attitudes, behaviors, actions and results makes it critical for the daily life of human beings. This loop pattern indicates that initiation point of Mindset which can eventually lead towards, attitudes which drive behaviors and then the actions. Actions can result in various different outcomes which will then determine the performance standards. The ever going loop infers that mindset initiates all our actions and results, yet the cycle will continue and can be subject to change. It means that depending upon a particular outcome and performance, the human mind has the ability to alter, modify and adapt a new mindset.

Some other determinants of mindset and related phenomenon relate to following major facts about mindset and its effect on our lives.

➢ Belief in relation to ability

Mindset denotes the set patterns of belief and vision. So the way you pursue this belief will eventually affect your ability to do a thing. If you have a negative mindset about mathematics, you will never be able to perform well. But if you believe that mathematics is boring but you will put up the effort to excel, you will ultimately do it. In this case, the mindset about mathematics as a subject is negative but the belief in your abilities is productive enough to make you put efforts. In the reverse case, if negative view about the subject, would have been accompanied by the negative belief about your abilities, you could never have done well in mathematics.

Hence, if your abilities are hindered or are not in use because of a particular mindset, then you need to change it.

➤ Mindset affects decisions

Just as your mindset affects your ability, it also affects your decisions. For example, in a workplace you may encounter different people, belonging to different nationalities and cultures. If you have a negative stereotype about any of these groups, you will treat the person accordingly and your decision will be based on that mindset. It is not necessary that the mindset may have taken a particular shape because of some experience; it can be just a thought or social condition. But the results will be obvious in both cases and there are chances that the decision will not be based on rational judgments.

Growth mindset and fixed mindset

These are the two types or approaches followed while forming the mindset. As the name for each denotes, they are almost contrary to each other.

In the case of fixed mindset, the brain sends certain signals which make up fixed beliefs and views. In a fixed mindset, people believe that inherited qualities and abilities are just the determinants of our success or abilities so it is the nature which controls all our abilities. If we consider the present day world full of challenges we can say that fixed mindset can be problematic. It can hinder your hidden potentials and talents which need a suitable and appropriate nurture.

In fixed mindset people see others growing and get threatened. Instead of worrying about their performance they leave everything, making success hard to achieve. In the case of fixed patterns of thoughts, the person usually indulges in hiding the flaws or performance gaps. In this way, the chances of improvement are largely diminished.

The growth mindset is entirely opposite to fixed one. It nourishes the abilities and talents and makes a person fulfill all the dreams, even in the presence of hurdles and challenges. Although growth mindset cannot make you achieve the things which are beyond human abilities, yet it can increase the chances of achieving a challenging goal. As the name denotes, a growth mindset is driven by a belief in development and enhancement, so these people will bring their weaknesses on the surface so that they can make them better. Mentoring and coaching can largely affect these people. They can be put to challenging tasks and difficult situations, with every new challenge, the person gets even better and eventually success becomes a part of his or her journey.

As the above picture demonstrates that growth mindset is not only useful for individual goals and achievements rather it is also helpful in increasing the momentum of the group and societal wellbeing. Driven by growth mindset we humans can achieve greater wellness and societal success. Having discussed these two mindsets, the next point which comes under consideration is to achieve success. No matter what type of mindset you have had for so many years, nature has blessed the humans with the capability to change it with deliberate effort and conscious attentions. When growth mindset is achieved, success will become even more obvious and illustrious.

Chapter 2: Mindset Tricks and Positive Thinking

As we have discussed in the previous section that mindset denotes our behaviors and eventual performance, so in order to be successful in all walks of life one needs to get attentive towards nourishing a positive mindset. It is only possible with growth mindset because fixed mindset will never guarantee success. It will hinder the effect of hard work and passion against challenges.

In this book, we will discuss 10 mindset tricks making positive thinking part of your life and connecting your way of struggle towards achievements and triumph.

1. Believe in yourself

2. Ensure peace of mind to generate power

3. Develop some constant sources of energy

4. Look for happiness all around

5. Expect the best and make it your benchmark

6. Don't believe defeat as an option

7. Break the habits of worrying all the time

8. Solve your problems at your own

9. Surround yourself with successful people

10. Use physical health to get emotional contentment

Now we will discuss these tricks with a special reference to positive thinking so that you can use them as a source of success

1. Nurture a Firm Believe in Yourself

One of the major disadvantages of fixed mindset is that people see their abilities just like those of programmed machines. They think that nature has sent them with fixed chip installation and they have to live with it. Genetics and hereditary play an important role, but an equal role is played by an accurate approach of nurture.

The first mindset trick is to tune up yourself with a strong commitment and consideration that you are able to do miracles. When you have such an approach you will definitely put effort for proving your belief. However, in the reverse case, the positive thinking which is needed to carry forward positive effort is missing and the results will eventually take you towards grief and sorrow.

In order to make up a strong belief in yourself, you can take following step by step approach for enhancing the output rate of your efforts.

➢ Perform a thorough analysis of your past, present and desired future.
➢ List down the highlighting features of all these stages and milestones which you want to achieve in future.
➢ List the abilities and competencies which will pave your way to get to these milestones.
➢ Highlight the deficiencies in your abilities and proficiencies.
➢ Work on deficiencies with an aim that you can achieve the highest possible level of those competencies.
➢ Do not consider objective performance measures, consider improvement as a triumph

It will also create a self-fulfilling prophecy under which you will do what you believe. In order to keep the face-up, you will stay firm and keep on trying. When you will try you will succeed and your belief will eventually prove to be true. It will keep on going like a cycle and you will start having positive thoughts about yourself. Wishing for success, with negative thoughts is like going for battleground without any weapon and thinking that you will kill the army.

Another important step in constructing a belief about yourself is to think about your achievements time and again. Think about those moments when you were really successful and it will lead you to carry along better success rate.

2. Ensure Peace of Mind to Generate Power

One of the critical reasons for becoming a victim of negative thoughts is the absence of peace, within one's self. The internal peace always plays a contributing factor in establishing the mindset with positive thoughts. The inside peace of mind determines the way a person reacts to different situations and faces the hurdles. If you want to become successful in every walk of life, try to develop the habits which can lead you towards a peaceful mind.

> ➤ **Stop over thinking**

Over thinking is much like a physical ailment. It captures your thoughts and attitudes in such a way that you are left with nothing. Although being analytical is a good thing, but there is a difference between positive thinking and over thinking. One of the greatest disadvantages of over thinking is that it leaves you impaired. You cannot put obvious and objective efforts for a goal when your mind is full of these over thinking patterns. Over thinking may result when you put extra focus on small details. It also happens when you want everything in some specific way.

➤ Leave the things which are beyond your control

Another major reason for the absence of mental peace is a desire for controlling things. Every human being has some physical and mental constraints which restrict him or her to put efforts beyond a specific level. While determining your level of success, when you set unrealistic goals, you become a victim of negative thinking. A wish to control your constraints or getting anxious about the things which are not in your control will never let you gain peace.

The best way to maintain a positive attitude towards success is to put up efforts at your best and then leave everything. Over thinking or considering yourself incapable will eventually convert your mindset towards a fixed approach and you will not be able to utilize your potentials to the fullest.

➤ Stop the comparisons- everyone is residing a different boat

One of the common reasons which have made our lives devoid of peace is the "undue comparisons". We see others as their achievements and success, without thinking the contextual factors. When an unrelated reference point is marked, you will never be able to go up to that mark. This inability will relate restlessness and agitation. Eventually, a restless mind will divert you towards negative thinking and success will get even far. Peace of mind will result from putting religious efforts at individual levels, without looking for comparisons.

Chapter 3: Energy and Happiness Need to Be Created

In this chapter, we consider two major tricks which can lead you automatically towards positive thinking so that the chances of getting successful are enhanced.

3. Develop some Constant Sources of Energy

Mindset is not innate; it is molded, adapted and reformed with every passing moment. You were not born with something called mindset, it was the environment and experience which fed your thoughts and governed your mindset. If your thoughts are continuously pulling you towards negative polls, it means that you are lacking some definite source of energy which is needed for positive thoughts and growth mindset. You can work on this energy source by considering the following aspects

➢ **Explore intrinsically and extrinsic motivation**

Motivation is a driving force; it is a source of up thrust and momentum which can keep you going towards success. One reason for being pessimistic is that we have surrounded ourselves with meaningless achievements. Everyone has certain intrinsic and extrinsic motivational sources. Look up for those sources. Some people are attracted towards money, other want recognition and accomplishment. Draw out precise sources which can motivate you.

> **Reward yourself**

Negative thoughts also emerge as a result of nonstop efforts and hectic ventures. No matter which type of success you want to achieve, it is essential that you reward yourself. This reward can be tangible as well as intangible; it can be something which you badly wish for or some words of appreciation for yourself. Rewards always tone you up for further effort. The reward is like an acknowledgment of the efforts put up by a person. When rewarded a person thinks of his efforts as fruitful so he/she eventually looks up towards the greater effort, this cycle will eventually end up towards the final destination.

> **Celebrate success**

Positive thoughts can emerge if you divide your venture into small episodes. Upon covering each milestone, you and your body both need celebration. Do not keep on longing for final destiny, whether it is related to some financial success or some workplace goal. Even a step ahead on the way should be celebrated well. The celebration may mean a cup of coffee with your loved ones, or a day out with your family. When celebrated, success becomes even more visible. The visible steps towards success journey will enhance your energy and you will look for further success even with greater efforts. This is especially critical when we have to cover a long way towards success, so in order to avoid boredom and pessimism, it is necessary to celebrate small steps towards the achievement.

4. Look for Happiness All Around

Positive thinking is driven with a positive approach towards life. People who have a habit to look for loopholes, flaws and weaknesses are never able to achieve a positive mindset. Filled with negativity, the human mind will never get a person towards happiness. A major rule for contended view about life is to look for happiness all around.

> ➢ **Do what pleases you**

When you are heading for some goal or challenge, always leave some space for yourself. Get some time for activities which is a source of pleasure for your mind and body. It will boost up your energy levels and you will always consider yourself energetic. If painting is your passion, get some time for it. If photography is what pleases you always assign some moments for photography. It will enhance the happiness within you and you will not become a victim of negative thoughts.

➤ Have a positive company

The man is no doubt a social entity. The ideas, beliefs and thoughts of a human being cannot remain aloof from the people who are dwelling around him. It is, therefore, necessary that you have that kind of people around you who are really having a positive charge. Negative people have a negative view of life and see the things from a darker side. They eventually take up the surrounding domains and anyone who has weak control over his or her mindset can become a victim of these people. When you are determined towards success, ensure that you have an army of positivity with you. This army will comprise of your own thoughts oriented positively, as well as people who have a positive orientation towards life. Get connected to people who can give you a good piece of advice.

Chapter 4: Expectation and Defeat are Closely Linked

In this chapter, we will discuss the typical connection of defeat and belief so that we can use it as a mindset trick against negative thoughts. The two tricks considered in this chapter are closely linked and they have a momentous effect in determining the eventual success.

5. Expect the Best and Make It Your Benchmark

While discussing mindset we discussed the fixed and growth mindset. The two types are parallel to each other based on their tendency to motivate a person. Under the fixed mindset, the outcomes are viewed as fixed, stereotypically determined, with no expectation of improvement. Under the influence of this mindset the person loses the insight of a situation and loses hope. One of the most useful tricks, in this case, is to shift the benchmarks to the opposite poles. If your negative thinking and fixed mindset is driving your thoughts towards losing hope, set the highest benchmark. When you start thinking from the lowest point then the distance required for reaching the highest point gets even longer. Expectation and the resulting behavior are tied together in the form of a loop.

So when you believe and dream bigger, you will act wider and more powerful. Eventually, success will become a destiny for you. When you start from the negative and worst point, the energy needed for motivation keeps on increasing its demands. You end up in giving up. Always make the struggle for the highest level of brightness and excellence.

6. Don't Believe Defeat as an Option

Positive thinking cannot flourish in the presence of negative lenses. The lenses which always focus on negative aspects including defeat will give you a darker picture of every situation. Defeat is encountered when it is known, do not make your mind a victim of negative thoughts, and get a mindset which can make you exert efforts for success. A positive mindset is not over confident. It just keeps a realistic view of the tendency of a person to become a victim of defeat. If you will be determined enough for getting success, you will never start your venture with defeat as an option. When this tendency is ruled out the effects of negative thoughts will be minimized.

> ➢ **Learn lessons**

Under this mindset trick, try to view defeat from a different perspective. Rather than labeling it as "defeat", try to view it as a lesson learned in life. It will enhance the capability of handling the defeat and weaknesses. A person with positive thinking will not repeat the defeat scenario because he or she will learn important lessons from defeat episode. A defeat becomes a real crush when it ceases your abilities to carry on your efforts.

➢ Focus on improvements

Never overwhelm your mind with the labels of "defeat". It will tune up your mind for this word and its aftermaths. The human mind put certain labels for certain scenarios and it acts like a verbal condition. Whenever a specific word is uttered, listened or read, it displays certain images and views in your mind. As a trick take away the word defeat from your mind and replace it with improvements and lessons. When you encounter certain unfavorable result, evaluate the causes which led you towards it and then next time avoid becoming a victim of the same situation. It is possible only when you have a focus towards improvements and enhancements.

➢ Do not hesitate to experiment

Defeat is usually a part of your course when you follow a typical path and have a fixed mindset. Change the mindset to growth category and try out new ways of doing things. Maybe defeat was the outcome of a particular course because it was done in a wrong way. Try to experiment different ways of doing things. Experiments can enhance your fresh thoughts. When you will do a work in a new and nonstereotypical way, the chances of getting caught by negative thoughts will be lesser.

Chapter 5: Problem-solving and Habit Making Drives the Course of Success

Actions can result in various different outcomes which will then determine the performance standards. The ever going loop infers that mindset initiates all our actions and results, yet the cycle will continue and can be subject to change. It means that depending upon a particular outcome and performance, the human mind has the ability to alter, modify and adapt a new mindset.

7. Break the Habits of Worrying All the Time

Another important hurdle in the way of positive thoughts is the tendency to remain worried all the time. You may have encountered many people around you who are labeled as "carefree". I think everyone should have a little bit of carefree soul in his or her inner being.

➢ Develop rational and logical thinking

One of the major reasons for having recurrent worry attacks is the lack of rational thinking. When we base our decisions and observations on illogical thoughts, they overcome our mind like a monster. Eventually, we become a victim of worry and depression. Worry is largely related to the ability to be successful. When undue depression is always on your mind, one cannot put extensive efforts for success. The undue wastage of energy (because of these worry attacks) will largely hinder the way of success.

➤ Feed your worries with positivity

In case you are having an overwhelming attack of worry, put deliberate efforts for making positive efforts. Like a physical body, cover your worries with a veil of positivity. Deliberately put efforts for finding positive connections in a particular aspect and situation.

➤ Keep away from stereotypes

Stereotypes are said beliefs and opinions about a situation, person or group. Although well established, these stereotypes may be the result of some eventual false belief. If you are viewing something stereotypically the chances of getting worry attacks are largely enhanced.

8. Solve Your Problems at Your Own

Another important trick to enhance the chances of beings successful is the ability of a person to solve the problems on their own. Problem-solving is a complex task, which requires in-depth analysis and eventual struggle. However many people because of their negative view about their abilities put others to solve their problems. This makes them kind of handicapped. Their ambiguity about their competencies makes them a negative thinker. Consequently, the result is just an increased frequency of failures.

➤ No one can put their feet in your shoe

When your mind pushes you towards availing the problem-solving abilities of someone else, think for a while. Think that everyone is different. No one can replace you. No one can feel your pain. People can be sympathetic, no doubt, but the real feelings are only experienced by the real actor. So instead of taking a risk, try for your own decision making. Maybe you may not get successful for the first time but even in the case of unfavorable results, you will get a chance to learn a lesson.

> ➤ **You are the master**

Another major way of getting into decision making is the belief that you are the master. This is again related to the positive thinking therapy, when you will have a belief, you will be ready for taking risks and trying harder for success. Another critical factor is the blame game. When you act on other's will and decision, you do not feel the real attachment with the decision. In this case, if you fail, you just put the blame on others and do not extend efforts for doing something good.

9. Surround Yourself With Successful People

Another mindset trick which we miss most of the time relates to contextual factor. No matter what dispositional factors you may possess, the role of contextual factors can never be denied. It is because of this reason that children with different nurture come out as different individuals. Human beings have the capacity to grasp lessons and findings from the surrounding. The surrounding also caters human models, their abilities, and attitudes. If you have a specific success criterion your mind, try to have the company of people who are good in that area. Their success will help you to achieve motivation and a belief that anything is possible with deliberate effort.

➢ Learn from their experience

Try to indulge in fruitful discussion. Ask them about the struggles and hard work which they had to put to gain this level of achieving. In this way rather than worrying or indulging in negative thoughts you will spend your time in fruitful discussion.

➢ Get advice

As these will be the people with success history, let them provide you the best piece of advice regarding achievements and success.

> ### Surround your mind with positive vibes

Although we are talking about successful people and their company, yet not every successful person will be the source of positivity and positive mindset. Beware of the people who may indulge you into negativity and illegal ways of achieving success. Look for people who are able to transmit positive vibes.

10. Use Physical Health to Get Emotional Contentment

Mindset may connote a cognitive part of a person's life, yet the connection between physical health and mental wellness can never be denied. It is a well-proven fact that if a person is having a healthy body, then the chances of becoming a victim of negative thoughts are largely reduced. The physical ailments and body problems can enhance the negative emotions. Under the stress of pain or disease, a person always goes for negative thinking.

> ### Body and mind are interwoven

Mental health is only possible when the body is nourishing under healthy circumstances. You can never see a person on the bed with some disease claiming that he is feeling enthusiastic. It is never possible. This interconnectivity demands that you pursue body health so that it can make you nourish a healthy mind. Only under the effect of healthy mind, you can develop positive thinking. Negativity prevails like an ailment and it becomes even greater with negative heath condition.

➢ Physical vigor enhances mental capacities

If a person is fresh and feels high levels of energy, the positive vibes are generated within the body and the person becomes inclined to put efforts for success. If you feel that you cannot put successive efforts for a goal, one reason can be your falling health. Although evaluative abilities come with mental strength but the physical effort needed to pursue a goal is only insured by a healthy body. Mindset can be focused with this view of physical health and the results will be phenomenal for achieving success.

Conclusion

The human mind can make up miracles and lead our way towards an ever increasing probability of success. The basis of human thoughts is connected to so many different parameters that one can not relate it to some specific rule of thumb. However, the researchers are putting extensive efforts for making up some useful discoveries for the enabling betterment of human life and societal wellbeing.

Mindset is one of the critical aspects which lead us towards eventual outcomes, both positive as well as negative. Based on the positive mindset the human race has made revolutions and miracles, in all fields of life, but nourishing a positive mindset is not an easy job. Sometimes driven by negativity, people lead miserable lives. This book will cater with the issue of developing positive mindset through utilizing the abilities of mindset. Using these tricks, you can cherish success in all fields of life. If you apply these tricks in your life, with a focus towards enhancing and developing your mindset, there are enough chances to get eventual success in all walks of life.